THE BEST YO MAMA JOKES

1.   Yo mama so fat...

a.   ...she sat on the beach and Greenpeace helped her back in the ocean!

2.   Yo mama so fat...

a.   ...that she has to wear blinkers whenever she goes out.

3.   Yo mama so old...

a.   ...that her driver's license is in hieroglyphics.

4.   You mama so ugly...

a.   ...that she freaks out blind people!

5. **Yo mama so fat...**

a. *...that she walked in front of the TV and I missed an entire show.*

6. **You mama so fat...**

a. *...that when she got baptized she had to do it at Seaworld!*

4

7. Yo mama so fat...

a. ...that she uses the highway as a waterslide.

8. Yo mama so poor...

a. ...that I walked into her house and I was immediately in the backyard.

9.   Yo mama so dumb...

a.   ...that she got stuck at the stop sign because it never turned green.

10.   Yo mama so dumb...

a.   ...that she threw out all the W's at the M&M factory.

11. Yo mama so fat...

a. *...that she sat next to everyone when she was in school!*

12. Yo mama so fat...

a. *...that you people throw coins in her bellybutton and make a wish.*

13.   Yo mama so fat...

a.   ...when she walked down the street in a yellow raincoat people thought she was a school bus!

14.   You mama so fat...

a.   ...that when a meteor hit her she thought it was a raindrop.

15.   Yo mama so dumb...

a.   ...that she put lipstick on her scalp to makeup her mind!

16.   You mama so poor...

a.   ...that when I stepped on a cigarette she asked, "Who turned out the lights?"

17.   Yo mama so fat...

a.   ...that it takes a year to go around her.

18.   Yo mama so fat...

a.   ...that everyone thought there was an earthquake when she rolled over in bed!

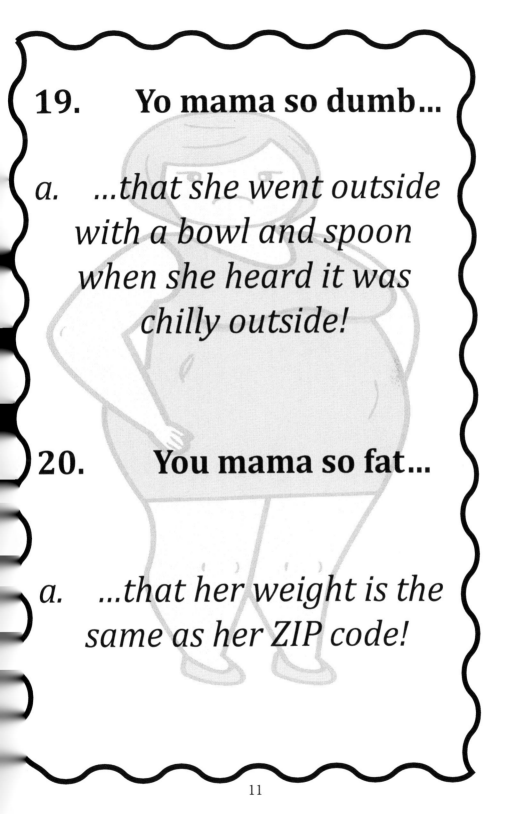

19.   Yo mama so dumb...

a.   ...that she went outside with a bowl and spoon when she heard it was chilly outside!

20.   You mama so fat...

a.   ...that her weight is the same as her ZIP code!

21.   Yo mama so fat...

a.   *...that she got lost in a photo booth.*

22.   Yo mama so dumb...

a.   *...that she got in a fight with a statue!*

23.   Yo mama so dumb...

a.   ...that she got in an accident when she got hit by a parked car!

24.   Yo mama so dumb...

a.   ...that she bought a free sample!

25.   Yo mama so old...

a.   ...that her social security number had one digit.

26.   Yo mama so dumb...

a.   ...that she walked around the house when someone told her Christmas was around the corner.

27.   Yo mama so dumb...

a.   ...that she got tangled in a cordless phone!

28.   Yo mama so dumb...

a.   ...that she thought Taco Bell was a phone company!

29.   Yo mama so dumb...

a.   ...that she went and got a ladder when I said drinks were on the house!

30.   Yo mama so fat...

a.   ...that she's the reason the Titanic sank!

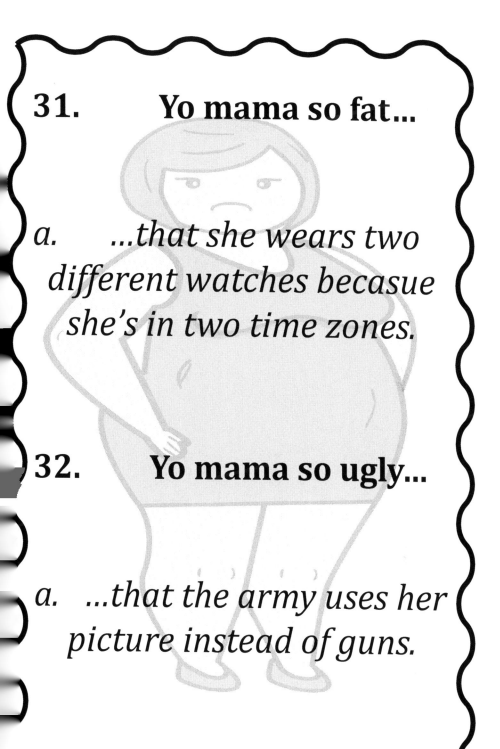

31.   Yo mama so fat...

a.   ...that she wears two different watches becasue she's in two time zones.

32.   Yo mama so ugly...

a.   ...that the army uses her picture instead of guns.

33. **Yo mama so ugly...**

a. *...that when she went to the haunted house, they offered her a job.*

34. **Yo mama so fat...**

a. *...that she has to take a pickup truck through the drive thru.*

35.   Yo mama so fat...

a.   ...that she got her ears pierced by a javelin.

36.   Yo mama so ugly...

a.   ...that a boomerang refused to come back when she threw it.

37.   Yo mama so dumb...

a.   *...that she asked where the Great Wall of China was!*

38.   Yo mama so fat...

a.   *...that she only knows 3 letters of the alphabet: K.F.C.*

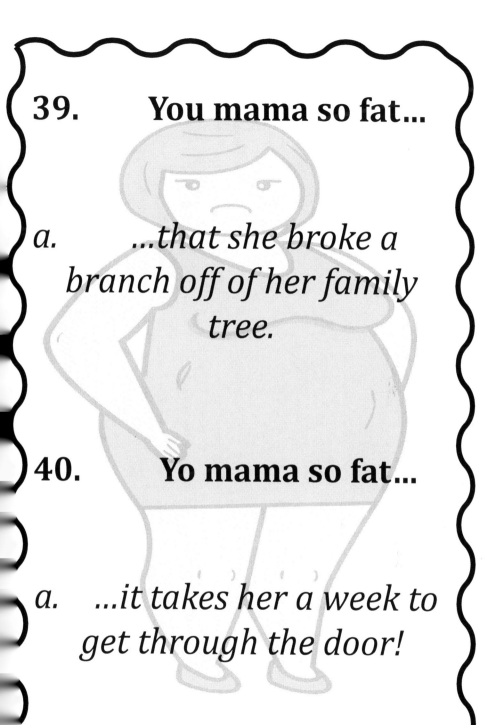

39.   You mama so fat...

a.   ...that she broke a branch off of her family tree.

40.   Yo mama so fat...

a.   ...it takes her a week to get through the door!

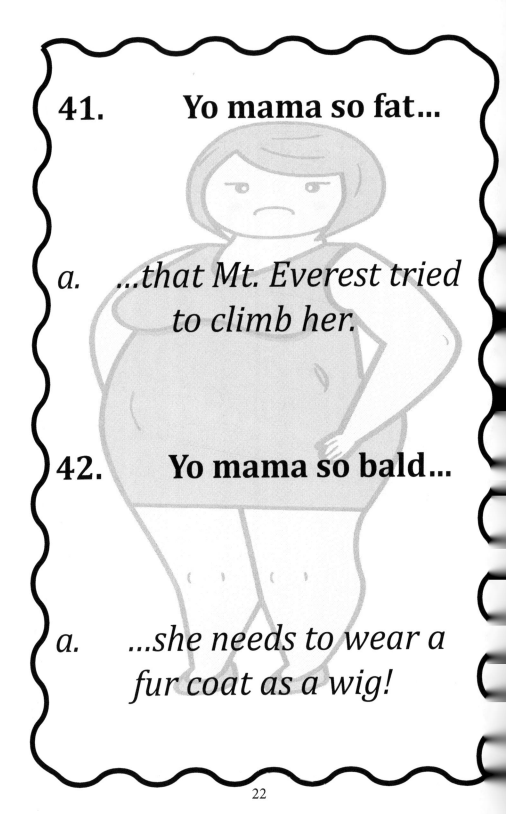

41.   Yo mama so fat...

a.   ...that Mt. Everest tried to climb her.

42.   Yo mama so bald...

a.   ...she needs to wear a fur coat as a wig!

43.   Yo mama so bald...

a.   ...that you can see what she's thinking about!

44.   Yo mama so smelly...

a.   ...that she makes onions cry

45.   *Yo mama so bald...*

a.   *...that her head slips off the pillow when she goes to bed.*

46.   **Yo mama so dumb...**

a.   *...that she studied an orange juice container all morning because it said "concentrate."*

47.   Yo mama so skinny...

a.   ...that we couldn't see her when she turned sideways.

48.   Yo mama so skinny...

a.   ...she uses a fruit loop as an inner tube.

49. **Yo mama so fat...**

a. *...that when she got in the ocean there was a tsunami warning!*

50. **Yo mama so dumb...**

a. *...she put a seatbelt on her computer to protect it if it crashed.*

51. **Yo mama so stupid...**

a. *...that she complained when her donut had a hole in it!*

52. **Yo mama so ugly...**

a. *...her parents needed to use a slingshot to feed her.*

53. Yo mama so fat...

a.   ...that she needs a whole team of painters to put on makeup!

54.   Your mama so dumb...

a.   ...that when I told her she lost her marbles she started looking for them.

55.   **Yo mama so dumb...**

a.   *...that when she was driving to the airport, she saw a sign that said "airport left," so she went home.*

56.   **Yo mama's so fat...**

a.   *...that she turns heels into flats.*

57.   Yo mama so dumb...

a.   *...she put a ruler in her bed to see how long she slept.*

58.   Yo mama so fat...

a.   *...that's more worldwide than the web.*

59.   Yo mama so dumb...

a.   ...that she thought the Super Bowl was where you put a lot of chili!

60.   Yo mama so fat...

a.   ...that she got her picture taken and it took a year to print!

61. Yo mama so fat...

a. ...that the bears hide food from her when she goes camping!

62. Yo mama so dumb...

a. ...that she tried to send a voicemail by yelling into the mailbox!

63. **Yo mama so dumb...**

a. *...when the judge said "Order in the court!" she asked for a burger and fries!*

64. **Yo mama so fat...**

a. *...that she makes King Kong look like a stuffed animal!*

65.   **Yo mama so fat...**

a.   *...that the aliens thought she was the mothership!*

66.   **Yo mama so fat...**

a.   *...that she turned her iPhone into an iPad just by sitting on it.*

67.   Yo mama so stupid...

a.   *...that she sold her car so she could get gas money!*

68.   Yo mama so fat...

a.   *...that you need a passport to get on her good side.*

69.   Yo mama so greasy...

a.   ...she used bacon as a bracelet!

70.   Yo mama so dumb...

a.   ...that she went to the dentist to fix her Bluetooth.

71. **Yo mama so fat...**

a. *...that she's unable to jump to conclusions!*

72. **Yo mama so fat...**

a. *...that she'll lower all the prices if she sits down in the store.*

73. Yo mama so fat...

a. ...that when she walks outside she causes an eclipse.

74. Yo mama so fat...

a. ...that if you think about her you'll break your neck.

75. Yo mama so fat...

a. ...that her bellybutton arrives home 20 minutes before she does.

76. Yo mama so dumb...

a. ...that when I asked for a hot pocket she lit my pants on fire!

77.   Yo mama so fat...

a.   ...that she causes an earthquake whenever she falls down.

78.   Yo mama so fat...

a.   ...that when she fell into a black hole, she clogged it!

79. **Yo mama so fat...**

a.   ...that when she steps on the scale it shows her phone number.

80.   Yo mama's teeth are so yellow...

a.   ...that when she smiled she caused traffic to slow down.

81. Yo mama so fat...

a. ...that little kids tried to ride her when she went to the circus.

82. Yo mama so old...

a. ...that her birth certificate expired.

83. **Yo mama so short...**

a.   ...that she uses a staple as a pullup bar.

84. **Yo mama so short...**

a.   ...that she drowned in a puddle.

85. **Yo mama so ugly...**

a. *...that she scared her reflection away!*

86. **Yo mama so ugly...**

a. *...even her imaginary friend wouldn't play with her.*

87. **Yo mama so fat...**

a. *...that her physician is Dr. Pepper.*

88. **Yo mama so fat...**

a. *...that when she wore a yellow raincoat people yelled "Taxi!"*

89. **Yo mama so poor...**

a.   ...that when I asked her why she was kicking a box, she said "moving."

90. **Yo mama so fat...**

a.   ...that her favorite basketball team is the Dunkin' Donuts.

91.   Yo mama so fat...

a.   ...that when she stepped on the scale it told her to get off.

92.   Yo mama so dumb...

a.   ...that she sits on the television and watches the sofa.

93. Yo mama so fat...

a. ...that whenever she sits in the back seat the car does a wheelie.

94. Yo mama so fat...

a. ...that when she gets her picture taken they need to use a satellite.

95. **Yo mama so fat...**

a. *...that her belt is as big as the equator.*

96. **Yo mama so ugly...**

a. *...that Freddy Krueger has nightmares about her.*

97.   Yo mama so dumb...

a.   ...she spent 5 hours trying to ask the mannequin where the sweaters were.

98.   Yo mama so fat...

a.   ...that she got an "A" in lunch.

99. Yo mama so fat...

a. ...that when she wears red people think she's the Kool-Aid Man.

100. Yo mama so fat...

a. ...that if you run one lap around her you've run a marathon.

Printed in Great Britain
by Amazon

14910259R00032